Department of Trade and Industry

TransTec plc

Investigation under Section 432(2) of the Companies Act 1985

Interim Report by Hugh Aldous FCA and Roger Kaye QC
(Inspectors appointed by the Secretary of State for Trade and Industry)

LD 2465524 4

LONDON: The Stationery Office

Published with the permission of the Department of Trade and Industry on behalf of the Controller of Her Majesty's Stationery Office.

© Crown Copyright 2001

All rights reserved.

Copyright in the typographical arrangement and design is vested in the Crown. Applications for reproduction should be made in writing to the Copyright Unit, Her Majesty's Stationery Office, St Clements House, 2-16 Colegate, Norwich NR3 1BQ.

First published 2001

ISBN 0 11 515495 7

LEEDS LIBRARY AND
INFORMATION SERVICES

X φ	
338.7	BI
GRE	6/3/01
S002083	Sub

Printed in the United Kingdom by The Stationery Office
TJ003577 C10 02/01 592453 19585

CONTENTS

Chapter		Page

Appendices

Hugh Aldous FCA and Roger Kaye QC

Inspectors appointed under s.432(2) of the Companies Act 1985 to investigate and report on the affairs of TransTec plc

22 January 2001

Rt Hon Stephen Byers MP
Secretary of State for Trade and Industry
1 Victoria Street
London
SW1H 0ET

Dear Sir,

TransTec plc

On 20th January 2000 you appointed us under section 432(2) of the Companies Act 1985 to investigate the affairs of TransTec plc. We are pleased to present our interim report to you under the provisions of section 437(1) of that Act.

You will recall it was initially anticipated that we might be able to submit a final report to you in a comparatively short period of time. For the reasons stated in the interim report we have not been able to achieve our initial optimistic target, but we believe, nevertheless, that the bulk of our work in terms of collection of evidence has been completed. However, as it is the anniversary of our appointment, and for other reasons stated in the report, we felt it appropriate to make this report to you now.

There are three points we wish to emphasise to you. First, as we state in our interim report, there is still further work to be done. Second, our current perception of the facts and events in the history of the TransTec group may, by the time of our final report, have changed and our statements should, therefore, be viewed as tentative or provisional. Third, we have deliberately sought to refrain from any criticism of any company, firm or individual in our interim report. It must be remembered that those persons who are likely to be criticised have

Correspondence should be addressed to the secretary to the inspectors:
Jeannie Okikiolu ACA
RSM Robson Rhodes, 186 City Road, London EC1V 2NU
Direct telephone: 020 7865 2197
Direct fax: 020 7865 2496

not, apart from during the course of interviews or (in one case) in general correspondence, been formally apprised of the criticisms which we may be minded to make, or given the opportunity to reflect on those potential criticisms and correct or explain any relevant point of substance likely to be prejudicial to them.

Yours faithfully

HUGH ALDOUS FCA   **ROGER KAYE QC**

CHAPTER 1: INTRODUCTION

Appointment

1.1   On 20 January 2000 we were appointed in the following terms as inspectors to investigate the affairs of TransTec plc ("TransTec"):

> "The Secretary of State for Trade and Industry in exercise of the powers conferred upon him by section 432(2) of the Companies Act 1985 hereby appoints Hugh Graham Cazalet Aldous FCA of 186 City Road, London EC1V 2NU and Roger Godfrey Kaye QC of 24 Old Buildings, Lincoln's Inn, London WC2A 3UP to investigate the affairs of TransTec plc and to report thereon in such manner as the Secretary of State may direct."

Background

1.2   On 29 December 1999 HSBC appointed partners of the firm of Arthur Andersen joint administrative receivers over TransTec and its subsidiaries. This event, unremarkable in the ordinary course of events, would have gone largely unnoticed but for three significant factors. First, the company concerned was publicly quoted on the Stock Exchange; second, its major shareholder and former chairman was a Mr Geoffrey Robinson MP, a former member of the Labour Government until December 1998 when he resigned over an unrelated matter; third, the collapse of the company was accompanied by rumours of undisclosed liabilities of US $18 million to Ford-Werke AG ("Ford"), a subsidiary of the well known US car manufacturing company and one of TransTec's major customers.

1.3   In announcing our appointment, the Secretary of State publicly indicated that he expected us to concentrate on three aspects: the reasons for the collapse; the $18 million Ford claim, and whether this (and various other matters) had properly been disclosed in the accounts and to the proper authorities.

1.4   In this context it is also as well to remember the scope of the section under which we were appointed, namely section 432(2) of the Companies Act 1985. This provides:

> "(2)   The Secretary of State may make such an appointment [of inspectors] if it appears to him that there are circumstances suggesting-
>
> (a)   that the company's affairs are being or have been conducted with intent to defraud its creditors or the creditors of any other person, or otherwise for a fraudulent or unlawful purpose, or in a manner which is unfairly prejudicial to some part of its members, or
>
> (b)   that any actual or proposed act or omission of the company (including an act or omission on its behalf) is or would be so prejudicial, or that the company was formed for any fraudulent or unlawful purpose, or
>
> (c)   that persons concerned with the company's formation or the management of its affairs have in connection therewith been guilty of fraud, misfeasance or other misconduct towards it or towards its members, or
>
> (d)   that the company's members have not been given all the information with respect to its affairs which they might reasonably expect."

1.5   Since TransTec was a quoted company, we have also considered paragraphs 9.1(a) and 9.2 of the Listing Rules in force at the relevant time. These stated:

"9.1   A company must notify the Company Announcements Office without delay of any major new developments in its sphere of activity which are not public knowledge which may:

(a) by virtue of the effect of those developments on its assets and liabilities or financial position or on the general course of its business, lead to substantial movement in the price of its listed securities;

......

9.2   Where to the knowledge of a company's directors there is such a change in the company's financial condition or in the performance of its business or in the company's expectation of its performance that knowledge of the change is likely to lead to substantial movement in the price of its listed securities, the company must notify to the Company Announcements Office without delay all relevant information concerning the change."

Interim Report

1.6   When we were first appointed it was envisaged that we should produce our report fairly speedily. It is now a year since we were appointed. For reasons we set out below our progress with our enquiries was somewhat inhibited due to factors beyond our practical control and as a result events have somewhat caught up with us. There is now already speculation of a Spring general election (though none, of course, has been announced at the date of writing).

1.7   For these reasons, and particularly because of the otherwise likely speculation that might involve Mr Robinson and the Government, we felt that it was right that we should make this interim report to the Secretary of State as to where we are with our enquiries well before any election campaign gets fully under way and in the knowledge that this interim report might well be published. It is important to emphasise, however, that although we have achieved much and can, with some reasonable optimism say that we can see the conclusion of these enquiries, this report is simply a statement as to the point we have now reached. We have made no formal or final findings as yet, nor do we make any criticisms (provisional or otherwise) of anyone in this interim report.

The Scope of Our Enquiries

1.8   TransTec was the holding company of a group of medium sized and small engineering companies with a considerable number of subsidiaries. The group carried on a variety of engineering and manufacturing businesses: supplying parts to the automotive industry, manufacturing plastic components for the consumer electronics and domestic products market, and precision cutting and measuring machines, including laser cutters, for the industrial sector. It had at least 20 significant operating units. From the early 1990s and increasingly so, the core of these businesses was the supply of parts to the automotive industry through its Automotive Division (particularly its metal casting operations, which after 1996 were claimed to be the largest in the UK).

1.9   The group had its origins in the Midlands. Its head office was, on its demise, located at the Birmingham Business Park. It operated, however, from a number of different geographical sites throughout England, Wales, and Northern Ireland as well as in the USA, Spain and Australia. It was substantially created in its modern form in May 1991 under the chairmanship of Mr Geoffrey Robinson MP who also owned a substantial quantity of shares. Mr Robinson ran the group as chairman and chief executive until November 1994 when he stood down as chief executive in favour of a Mr Richard Carr, newly recruited to take over that post. Mr Robinson remained non-executive chairman until May 1997, when he left to take up a post in the new Labour government.

1.10   The group operated until 1999, when it ran into financial difficulties. It entered into negotiations with its lenders to secure additional funding. In December 1999 there was publicly revealed a claim by, and settlement of that claim with, Ford. The quantum of the settlement was said to be US $18 million. Following this disclosure the negotiations with the lenders effectively failed and the group began to be placed in administrative receivership on 29 December 1999.

1.11   It was clear to us from the outset that we needed to obtain information over a wide area, both in terms of geography and topics. We would need to obtain and see a large number of documents. We would also need to see a large number of people.

Difficulties with Our Enquiries

1.12   Nevertheless, we were initially optimistic that the scope and focus of our enquiries ought not to, and would not take us very long. We originally estimated that it might take us six to nine months. In part this was based on an early impression (substantially justified) that the group was very centrally organised and run with regular reports from the subsidiaries, or sites, to the central head office. Also in part this was based on an appreciation of our powers to extend our investigations to the subsidiaries (see section 433 Companies Act 1985) and of the duties of all relevant persons to co-operate with us (see section 434 and *Re An Inquiry into Mirror Group Newspapers plc* [2000] Ch. 194).

1.13   Unfortunately, we did not obtain anything like the full complement of documents we anticipated until mid-April to mid-May 2000, with a further amount being delivered to us by TransTec's administrative receivers ("the receivers") in July 2000. This set us back in our initial investigations by some three to four months. In the meantime our representatives were able to attend at the head offices of TransTec and to trawl through a number of files and documents with a view to an early identification of those which were likely to be of relevance and importance to our enquiries. In addition, although we were able to conduct some early interviews on the basis of such information as we obtained, this delay in obtaining documentation set us back considerably in even commencing a review of the full scope of our investigations. Once obtained, we then faced the mammoth task of organising and copying the documents into a manageable form. In some measure this delay may have been due to the fact that the receivers of TransTec and of the various subsidiaries had to cover much of the same ground as ourselves, particularly in relation to the Ford claim.

The Current State of Our Enquiries

1.14   To date we have interviewed 34 witnesses on oath, obtained statements from another 13 witnesses and reviewed documentation organised in some 100 lever arch files, being a digest of records and documents obtained from TransTec and other persons. This digest was based on the following: from Arthur Andersen (on behalf of the receivers) we received some 100 lever arch files of copy documents, 70 boxes of original TransTec records, a computer-readable copy of information on TransTec's computers and servers, and 5 lever arch files of notes of interviews with witnesses; from PricewaterhouseCoopers we were provided with some 100 files of audit working papers; from TransTec's brokers, Dresdner Kleinwort Benson (as they were formerly known): some 5 or 6 boxes of paper and lever arch files of original records; from Close Brothers: some 18 files of original records; and from Ford we received some 10 lever arch files of documents. We have also been assisted by information from the group's other advisers and other parties with whom the group had dealings as well as some expert assistance from the automotive industry. We have also received letters from Members of Parliament and members of the public.

1.15   We were also able ourselves to visit TransTec's head office in Birmingham. We also visited Campsie, Northern Ireland, where the SOHC (single overhead camshaft) cylinder heads were manufactured for Ford. This we did in April 2000 and have to record our appreciation of our visit and all the willing assistance and co-operation we received from the staff there, in particular from Ms Sinead McCurry, the plant manager who made our visit both welcome and informative.

1.16   We still have some matters to investigate, some to complete and some witnesses to see or see again, and further documentation to review and analyse. Additionally, it will be obvious from this interim report that many questions still remain apparently unanswered. Not least amongst these is the role of the auditors and directors. Since we are still interviewing representatives from the auditing firm and have not completed our interviews of the directors (as well as for the reasons set out in paragraph 1.7 above) we felt that it would not be fair or right, at this stage, to set out these matters in any detail.

1.17   In the main our enquiries have tended to concentrate on the following areas:

(a)   the causes and reasons for the collapse of the group;

(b)   the Ford claim referred to in paragraphs 1.2 and 1.10 above and the disclosure of that claim and its treatment in the accounts of the group;

(c)   various potential accounting irregularities including the nature and accounting treatment of a payment of £400,000 made by or on behalf of TransTec or of one or more of its subsidiaries to Rover in July 1997;

(d)   an alleged shortfall in the employees' pension fund of Earby Light Engineers Ltd ("Earby"), a subsidiary of TransTec.

1.18   Time wise, as will be apparent from the later chapters, we have tended to concentrate on the period 1993-1999 when most of the events relevant to the collapse of TransTec either took place or had their generation.

CHAPTER 2: THE TRANSTEC GROUP

The TransTec Business

2.1   We set out in Chapter 1 (paragraphs 1.8-1.10) the nature and extent of the business of the TransTec group. We now turn to deal, a little more fully, with the history of this group.

Formation and Early Years 1911-1991

2.2   On 28 March 1911 the company which eventually became known as TransTec was incorporated. In May 1991 the company was based in the Midlands with interests in engineering. The company was then known as Central & Sheerwood PLC ("C&S"). Its then chairman was the late Mr Robert Maxwell. He and his interests owned about 21 per cent of the issued share capital. Other then directors included Mr Robert Maxwell's son, Kevin, and also Mr Geoffrey Robinson, a businessman and the Member of Parliament for Coventry (North West). C&S purchased a company called Transfer Technology Ltd from Mr Robinson. This company had been started by Mr Robinson in 1981 in order to exploit commercially engineering research undertaken by British universities. By May 1991 the company owned a number of specialist engineering subsidiaries. At the same time as acquiring Transfer Technology Ltd, C&S acquired some additional engineering companies and businesses operating under the aegis of Mr Robert Maxwell or his interests.

Restructuring and Expansion 1991-1994

2.3   Following these acquisitions, a restructuring of the group was carried out leading to the basis of its last format. C&S changed its name to Transfer Technology Group PLC. Mr Robinson became chairman and chief executive officer of the newly named group. The Maxwells sold their 21 per cent holdings to institutional investors and resigned their directorships, ending their links with the group. Mr Robinson was left the biggest single individual shareholder.

2.4   Mr Robinson remained chairman and chief executive of the group from May 1991 to November 1994. Under his chairmanship the group acquired a number of new subsidiaries including BEW (Auto Products) Ltd (1992) ("BEW"), Earby (1992), and Fenworth Ltd (1993) ("Fenworth"). It embarked upon new projects, notably the supply of SOHC cylinder heads to Ford, a project probably destined to have calamitous consequences for the company and group. New faces came on board. Included amongst them were Mr Neil Logue, a chartered accountant with Coopers & Lybrand Deloitte and who, in that capacity, had been involved in the acquisition of Transfer Technology Ltd. He joined the restructured group at the end of May 1991 and became finance director. Mr Richard Rimington, also a chartered accountant, had been a non-executive director of C&S since 1987. He became non-executive deputy chairman. Mr William Jeffrey, also a chartered accountant with Coopers & Lybrand Deloitte, joined the group in June 1992 as financial controller reporting to Mr Logue (whom he succeeded as finance director in 1995 after Mr Logue left). Mr Rhys Williams joined the board in May 1993 as a non-executive director. He had been a director of GEC, Chairman of the Marconi group and of Radstone Technology plc and Pro Chancellor of the University of Warwick.

2.5   In May 1991 the revised structure of Transfer Technology Group plc broadly consisted of four operational divisions, Automotive, Metal Detection, Control Technology and Polymer Technology.

2.6   The Automotive Division consisted of two old C&S subsidiaries: A L Dunn & Co Ltd ("A L Dunn") and Coventry Apex Engineering Company Ltd ("Coventry Apex"). A L Dunn was a Nuneaton based company which had been formed in the early part of the 20th century. In the post war years it developed an aluminium gravity casting capability supplying the expanding automotive industry. It supplied Ford and was well regarded by them. Coventry Apex was a Coventry based company also supplying machining castings and other sub-contract work for the automotive industry. Both companies were operationally placed within TransTec's Automotive Division.

2.7   The Metal Detection Division contained a number of companies which manufactured electronic metal detection equipment used to screen for metallic foreign bodies in the food and pharmaceutical industries.

2.8   The Polymer Technology Division contained a number of companies which manufactured seals, rubber sheeting and extrusions and mouldings.

2.9   The Control Technology Division was responsible for the manufacture of measuring and scanning equipment used to control manufacturing processes. It represented the core business originally started by Mr Robinson in Transfer Technology Ltd.

2.10   In October 1993 Transfer Technology Group plc underwent a further change of name, this time to that with which it remained, namely TransTec plc.

2.11   In November 1994 Mr Robinson felt it was time to move to a back seat in TransTec. It was decided to recruit a new full-time chief executive. The short-listed candidates were three: Mr Richard Carr, a chartered accountant with a successful track record of acquisitions in the USA for the Tomkins Corporation, Dr Peter Summerfield, a chartered engineer with experience both in the aircraft industry and Rover, and Mr Tony Kirkman, also a chartered engineer with considerable experience in the GEC Avery Group. Mr Carr got the job, but Dr Summerfield and Mr Kirkman were also recruited as directors shortly after Mr Carr's appointment, as respectively, Divisional Managing Director of the Manufacturing Division, and Divisional Manufacturing Director of the Controls Division.

Expansion, Decline and Fall 1994-1999

Overview

2.12   The period 1994 to 1999 may perhaps be summarised shortly as one of continued expansion by acquisition accompanied by increasing reported turnover, followed by sharp decline in the first half of 1999. In fact what lay behind this picture was another one: declining gross margins from 1997 onwards, negligible operating profits after 1997, falling sales volumes in the second half of 1998, increasing borrowing, problems with Ford, and ultimate collapse. As 1998 progressed into 1999 there also emerged customer dissatisfaction with the quality and supply of parts and service across the group. Much of the group's problems seem to have been due to increasing its dependence on supply to the automotive industry at a time when that industry itself was changing rapidly in a move to cut costs.

2.13   Throughout this period the board of directors of the company consisted of a mix of executive and non-executive directors.   The dominant figures throughout the period, however, appear to have been Mr Carr and Mr Jeffrey.   Initially, Dr Summerfield had been quite closely involved in group management but he left in November 1997.   Mr Kirkman too resigned, in December 1998.   Mr Richard Parkin, a former audit manager with Coopers & Lybrand where he had worked on the TransTec audits and who had joined the company as financial controller in 1995, came to act increasingly on behalf of Mr Jeffrey throughout 1998 when the latter began to spend more time in Australia.   He eventually succeeded Mr Jeffrey as finance director of TransTec in March 1999.

2.14   Following the appointment of Mr Carr, Mr Robinson remained non-executive chairman until 6 May 1997 when he resigned on his appointment as HM Paymaster General in the new Labour government.   He was succeeded as non-executive chairman by Mr Rimington on an interim basis (Mr Rimington was by then in his 70s) until June 1998 when Mr Colin Cooke, the non-executive chairman of Fenner plc and a former chairman of Triplex Lloyd plc became the new non-executive chairman of TransTec.

2.15   Between November 1994 and 24 December 1999, when the board of TransTec decided that it could no longer continue to run the group, the directors and company secretary were as set out below (**Table A**).

Table A

TransTec directors and company secretary November 1994 to 24 December 1999

	Appointed	Resigned
Executive directors		
Dr Sami Ahmed	May 1991	December 1994
Mr Neil Logue	May 1991	January 1995
Dr Peter Summerfield	November 1994	November 1997
Mr Tony Kirkman	November 1994	December 1998
Mr Richard Carr	November 1994	December 1999
Mr William Jeffrey	August 1995	December 1999
Mr Richard Parkin	March 1999	-
Non-executive directors		
Mr William Hayden	June 1993	June 1996
Mr Geoffrey Robinson *	July 1987	May 1997
Mr Richard Rimington	June 1987	June 1999
Mr Rhys Williams	May 1993	-
Mr Colin Cooke	May 1998	-
Mr Robert Muddimer	July 1998	-
Company secretary		
Mr Ron Codrington	February 1992	

* an executive director from July 1987 to November 1994

Group Structure

2.16   The business of the group was ostensibly controlled by the board of TransTec downwards through a mix of divisional or operational structures and isolated subsidiary companies or geographical sites.

2.17   Following the restructuring of the group in May 1991 and the acquisitions of 1991-1996 the group underwent further restructuring. By mid 1999 the operational structure was broadly as described below.

2.18   The two principal operating divisions were the Manufacturing and the Controls Divisions. The former consisted of the Automotive Division, eventually renamed TransTec Engineered Products, and the Plastics and Rubber Division. The Automotive Division was itself subdivided into Casting, Machining and two Spanish companies, Construcciones Radio Electro-Mecanicas Sistemas de Automocion SL ("CREMSA") and Estampaciones Noroeste SA ("ENSA") acquired in January 1998. Casting consisted of A L Dunn at Nuneaton, BSK Aluminium Ltd (acquired July 1996) at Bourne, Droitwich (two sites), Oldbury, and in Wales, and TransTec Automotive (Campsie) Ltd ("TransTec Camspie"), which produced the SOHC cylinder heads for Ford at Campsie, Northern Ireland. Machining consisted of Coventry Apex at Coventry, Fenworth at Stroud, BEW at Rochester, and a further BSK site also in Coventry at Red Lane. To this group was added an Australian subsidiary, Farnell & Thomas Ltd, acquired in February 1998.

2.19   As we have seen, in November 1994 Dr Summerfield headed the Manufacturing Division and Mr Kirkman the Controls Division. In 1993 along with the acquisition of Fenworth came Mr Peter Munday, a director and major shareholder of that company. Mr Munday was given the title chairman of the Automotive Division until he retired in May 1998. Between November 1997 and May 1998 Mr Munday effectively took over Dr Summerfield's operational responsibilities. Following Mr Munday's retirement Mr Robert MacKenzie was appointed managing director of the Automotive Division in which position he remained until the collapse of the group. Mr MacKenzie had previously been managing director of Knight Wendling Ltd, a consulting firm which had provided advisory services to TransTec in connection with the SOHC project for Ford. Despite their titles, neither Mr Munday nor Mr MacKenzie were ever appointed main board directors of TransTec. Mr Munday was, however, a director of a subsidiary company, TransTec Campsie.

2.20   By 1999 the central management team comprised Mr Carr, Mr Jeffrey, Mr MacKenzie and Mr Parkin. Mr Carr and Mr Jeffrey seem to have remained particularly close. Their head office team also included a Mr Tony Sartorius and a Mr Philip London, both accountants, who dealt with a range of financial management and accounting issues, and a Mr Chris Snazell, who was head of marketing.

Operational Structures

2.21   For most of the period under review, the group was a collection of operating subsidiaries, each with one or more sites, ostensibly controlled by a small head office team. In 1998 there were at least 20 significant operating units or sites. Even in December 1999 some 28 subsidiary receivership appointments were made. Over the top of the subsidiary companies was laid divisional management, which reported to head office. The recording of transactions remained local by subsidiaries or sites. The head of each division (Dr Summerfield and Mr Kirkman when they were there) produced reports for the chief executive, Mr Carr, who in turn produced his own reports for the TransTec board meetings. Mr Jeffrey (and latterly Mr Parkin) produced a separate finance report for the board.

2.22   As a consequence, the main board was given its information largely by Mr Carr, Mr Jeffrey and Mr Parkin, with sometimes some divisional input by someone in attendance. Dr Summerfield was a main board director and did have direct knowledge of operational matters on the Automotive side until he left in November 1997 and Mr Kirkman was a main board director with direct knowledge of the Controls side until he resigned in December 1998. Aside from these, the main board, and, in particular, the non-executive directors and chairmen, appear to have been, in the main, wholly dependent on these three for their information.

2.23   The manner in which this operational and reporting structure in fact worked appears to have resulted in the main board not always being comprehensively informed. It also appears to have led to what some outsiders might have perceived to be some confusion over direct contractual relationships with customers, i.e. precisely with which TransTec group company they were dealing. These features have recurred during our inquiry and continue to be a subject of our investigation. We propose to deal with these matters more fully in our final report as well as with the duties, roles and responsibilities of the directors and managers and the implications for good and proper corporate governance.

2.24   The reported results of the group showed increased and increasing sales over the period 1993 to 1999 as set out below (**Table B**).

Table B

Summary of Key Group Financial Indicators
for years 1993 to 1998 and half year 1999 (£'000)

	1993	1994	1995	1996	1997	1998	1999 (half year)
Profit and loss							
Turnover	145,411	185,186	210,959	259,764	349,529	389,926	150,079
Gross margin - per cent	25%	14%	18%	22%	20%	17%	n/a
Operating profit/(loss)	12,329	(10,966)	8,757	16,185	19,981	464	(3,103)
Cashflow							
Operating cashflow	14,679	2,265	14,367	21,054	17,328	17,508	6,147
Net cashflow	463	(7,717)	(243)	33,942	(27,298)	7,811	(12,333)
Gearing - per cent	24%	90%	78%	31%	57%	66%	83%
Balance sheet							
Total fixed assets	27,735	27,362	40,111	67,661	86,444	129,769	130,253
Shareholders funds :							
Share capital & premium	33,374	33,989	39,704	102,355	111,667	119,181	119,181
Reserves	229	(13,405)	(11,152)	(45,208)	(41,021)	(36,474)	(42,737)
Total shareholders' funds/net assets	33,603	20,584	28,552	57,147	70,646	82,707	76,444

Note : All figures taken from statutory accounts
n/a - Figure not available from half year accounts

2.25   However, the majority of this growth was as a result of the process of acquisitions begun under Mr Robinson which continued under Mr Carr. Otford Manufacturing Ltd, a plastic injection moulding company was acquired (November 1995) and became part of a restructured Plastics and Rubber Division along with the Vector Plastics Group (Rolinx Ltd, Elliott Plastic Components Ltd and L&P Plastics Ltd) which manufactured plastic injection moulded components (June 1997). BSK Holdings Ltd and its subsidiaries, including BSK

Aluminium Ltd, a group of aluminium pressure and gravity die-casting and machining companies, was acquired in July 1996 and added to the Automotive Division. To this Division was also added Preconomy Ltd (February 1997) a tool maker servicing the aluminium die-casting and plastic injection moulding industries, and two Spanish automotive component manufacturing companies, CREMSA and its wholly owned subsidiary ENSA (January 1998). The last acquisition made by TransTec appears to have been a substantial stake in an Australian quoted company, Farnell & Thomas Ltd, which manufactured cast products.

The SOHC Project

2.26   In about 1993 Ford developed a new single overhead cam (SOHC) engine for use in its Ford Explorer, a best selling vehicle in the USA. Each SOHC engine contained two cylinder heads. Ford's plant at Cologne, Germany, won the manufacture of the engine, based in part on the low quoted price it had obtained from A L Dunn, which was one of Ford's favoured suppliers. The engines were to be assembled in Cologne and shipped to the USA for assembly in the Explorer vehicle. Following a lengthy period of competitive tender, comparison and investigation, A L Dunn won the contract in principle for the sole source supply of the new SOHC cylinder heads for Ford in November 1993. A L Dunn had quoted a price of $46 per cylinder head, some $23 cheaper than the other seriously considered bidder.

2.27   This was, on paper, a good and notable achievement for the group. It was also to be the largest single project that TransTec had so far undertaken. Although it had been A L Dunn which secured the business, TransTec management were not satisfied that Nuneaton had sufficient resources or capacity for the required production levels (initially a daily production volume of 2,700 heads, subsequently increased to 3,100). A new facility was thought to be necessary. Several options were considered and eventually a new site, at Campsie, in Northern Ireland, was selected on which to build a fully automated new production facility. Between 1994 and 1995 TransTec built a new foundry at Campsie to produce the cylinder heads. On 1 March 1994, a new company, TransTec Foundries Ltd, was incorporated as the vehicle for this purpose as a subsidiary of A L Dunn. On 11 April

1995 this company changed its name to TransTec Automotive (Campsie) Ltd, (i.e. TransTec Campsie). One of the major considerations in selecting the site in Northern Ireland was the availability of major grants from the Northern Ireland Industrial Development Board. The decision to base operations in Campsie was possibly critical and, in the event, probably was also to prove calamitous. These are matters, however, on which we have yet to reach a firm and final view.

2.28 The project was not the hoped for success. This is not the place for a detailed analysis. Suffice to say for present purposes there was a myriad of problems: delays, labour problems, the robots would not work efficiently or at all, the cylinder heads themselves underwent a design change, there were defects in quality, high scrap levels and other problems. All this, together with other factors, contributed to mounting costs and, no doubt, to increased frustration. TransTec was unable to supply Ford with enough cylinder heads of suitable quality and on time. This, in turn, according to Ford, caused or contributed to, delays in the production of engines at Cologne and consequential problems in the USA.

2.29 In July 1996 Ford issued its first formal "default of supply" letter to TransTec. By September 1996 (when it had been projected that full production would commence) it became clear that the robots could still not produce the volume required by Ford. The decision was taken to remove the automation and resort to manual casting of the aluminium cylinder heads. One consequence was a huge increase in untrained labour force at Campsie. The original business plan had called for a workforce of some 243 persons, but the resort to manual labour led to a peak labour force of over 750.

2.30 Throughout late 1996 and early 1997 Ford continued to inform TransTec of their dissatisfaction with the quality and number of cylinder heads shipped to Cologne. They announced that they intended to seek a second source and eventually contracted with Teksid, in Italy, to produce about half their requirement. They made it plain they would wish to seek compensation (whether or not they could legally succeed in doing so was another matter) for consequential losses. These were not initially pursued since the project was still in its infancy and they wished to encourage, rather than dispirit, TransTec Campsie.

2.31   At the beginning of 1997 Ford's attitude hardened, partly, it would seem, as a result of published articles emphasising the financial strength of TransTec in connection with its desire to pursue further acquisitions. On 23 April 1997 Ford sent a letter to TransTec setting out the main elements of alleged losses totalling some US $100 million. They indicated that they wished TransTec to reimburse them for costs at the Cologne engine plant amounting to some US $36 million. Offers and counter-offers, discussions and debate between Ford and officials from TransTec continued throughout the summer until August 1997 when the claim was settled on terms that involved TransTec paying Ford US $18 million in compensation over a three year period, mostly in quarterly instalments ending in 1999. The eventual method of payment was that Ford deducted each instalment from its trading account with each of four TransTec sites or subsidiaries which supplied Ford with components. Each deduction was documented by a debit note from Ford to the relevant site or subsidiary. The wording of these debit notes was the subject of some debate between Ford and TransTec in September 1997. The fact of the claim and its settlement, and the terms of the settlement and manner of payment were not formally reported to the board of TransTec (and in particular the non-executive directors) before December 1999.

2.32   Although attempts were made in 1997 and 1998 to improve production at TransTec Campsie and although such attempts did meet with some success, the Campsie plant was never profitable. In 1998 Mr MacKenzie negotiated a price increase with Ford and achieved success on this front in 1999, back dated to 1 January 1999. This was not, however, sufficient to make Campsie viable.

2.33   In 1999 the strategy for the production layout at Campsie was reviewed and plans laid for the supply of new carousel robotic equipment from FATA Aluminium, a division of FATA Group S.p.A, of Italy. That equipment was in the process of being agreed and installed when TransTec went into receivership.

2.34   We have tentatively drawn two conclusions from an analysis of the factors contributing to the expansion of the group between 1993 and 1999.

2.35   First, that the result of these acquisitions together with the new SOHC project being carried out at Campsie, Londonderry by TransTec Campsie, shifted the emphasis of the group into dependence on the automotive market at a time of increasing global competition, world wide over capacity, and declining markets. TransTec's biggest customers became Ford, Rover and, to a lesser extent, AlliedSignal. This increased dependence can be illustrated by comparing the turnover of the Automotive/Manufacturing Division with that of Controls as shown below (**Table C**).

Table C

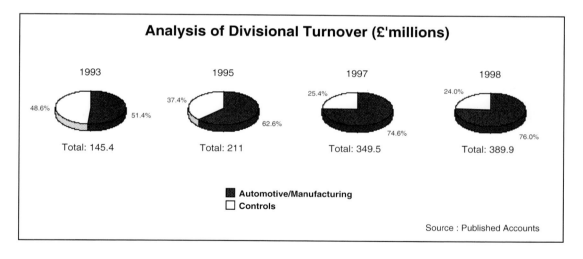

2.36   This dependence on the automotive market may itself have influenced the decline of TransTec. UK based suppliers were affected by a strong pound. Major manufacturers required higher quality and more reliable delivery. There was also a constant demand for competitive price reductions to be given by the suppliers - a process generally known in the trade as "cost downs" or sometimes as "economics". Manufacturers would expect 3 per cent, 4 per cent, or 5 per cent cost reductions year on year. They had the perceived (if not the actual) buyer power to achieve and enforce their demands. TransTec, in common with other suppliers, was affected by this process.

2.37 Secondly, the reported growth in turnover of the group was significantly contributed to by the acquisitions as well as organic growth. This can be seen from **Table D** below which shows an analysis of the turnover split between organic growth and growth attributable to these acquisitions.

Table D

Organic Growth against Acquisitions (£'000)

Year	Organic Growth	Acquisitions	Total Growth
1993	6,279	32,261	38,540
1994	35,682	4,093	39,775
1995	22,712	3,061	25,775
1996	19,696	29,109	48,805
1997	55,186	34,579	89,765
1998	(5,197)	45,594	40,397
Total	**134,358**	**148,697**	**283,057**

2.38 Further analysis of the reported figures that we have so far completed suggests also the following:

(a) A serious decline in turnover began in the second half of 1998. Whilst the entire group was affected, the largest fall was felt in the Automotive Division. To some extent this may be attributed to a decline in volumes of components requested by Ford and Rover, TransTec's two major automotive customers;

(b) There was a sharp fall in gross margin in 1994, after which it rose slightly in 1996 and then fell steadily away. After June 1998, turnover, margins and profitability declined, the latter due to the fall off in turnover and an increase in administrative expenses;

(c)   The subsidiary formed to operate the Campsie foundry, TransTec Campsie, never showed a profit. Indeed the growth in profit reported by the group between 1994 and 1998 (attributable substantially to the acquisitions) was then held back by the performance of TransTec Campsie. Between 1994 and 1998 the total reported pre-tax losses for TransTec Campsie were £20.3 million. It is our provisional view that these losses were almost certainly much greater for reasons appearing in Chapter 3 (paragraph 3.8) and Chapter 4 (paragraph 4.2);

(d)   The acquisitions also had a significant effect on cashflow. The acquisition of BSK Holdings Ltd in 1996 was funded by a rights issue, but the reported cash position in 1997 deteriorated as funds were used up on further acquisitions and capital expenditure. By 1998 TransTec's share price had declined to the extent that its shares could no longer be readily used to finance further acquisitions. After 1996 the net borrowings of the group increased. The acquisition of CREMSA and ENSA involved an increase in borrowing of £18.8 million. Despite raising cash of £30 million through the sales of businesses in 1998, by early 1999 the cash position of the group was very tight. The group was struggling to meet repayment commitments and by 30 June 1999 its reported net debt had risen to £66.5 million;

(e)   Excluding the amounts retained by Ford under the debit note system to which we refer in paragraph 2.31 above and discuss in more detail in Chapter 3, the total cash outflow from TransTec Campsie alone was £29.9 million. Most of this was attributable to 1996 and 1997 when production levels were low and capital investment in setting up the plant to manufacture and produce the SOHC cylinder heads was high. The amounts retained by Ford under the debit note system represented a further £7.2 million in 1997 and 1998 resulting in a total estimated cash outflow on Campsie of some £37.1 million.

Fall

2.39   From mid to late autumn 1998 onwards, the group made a number of attempts at refinancing. Despite a sale of the group's Measurement business (part of the Controls Division) in

December 1998, by mid 1999 the group's bankers were becoming concerned at the increased and increasing level of borrowing illustrated by the following table (**Table E**):

Table E

Net Borrowings

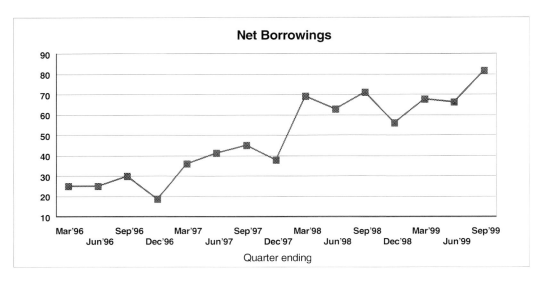

2.40   The matter was referred for special attention within the group's major lenders, HSBC. A lending group was put together, led by HSBC and comprising the TransTec group's principal lenders, HSBC, The Royal Bank of Scotland plc, First National Bank of Chicago (representing US loan note holders), and other banks that had assisted with the acquisition of CREMSA and ENSA. It soon became clear that TransTec would breach covenants in its borrowing agreements. In August 1999 the lending group appointed Arthur Andersen to review the situation and report to them. In September, facilities were further extended but only after taking debenture security. Hitherto lenders had been satisfied with cross guarantees from group companies without "hard" security. In October 1999, the group itself appointed Close Brothers and PricewaterhouseCoopers to advise on recovery and disposal.

2.41   The second half of 1999 saw close monitoring of the group by the lenders and a range of advisers. All advisers seem to have agreed on the group's need for increased facilities.

Following a review of the group's position and strategy by Arthur Andersen, group management decided to sell the group's businesses. The only alternative seemed the appointment of receivers. To achieve the necessary cash flow to enable the group to survive during the period of sell off TransTec negotiated with the lenders, led by HSBC, for additional limited term finance.

2.42   In mid-December 1999 it emerged that the non-executive directors, the auditors, the advisers, the brokers and the Stock Exchange had not been made aware of the existence and settlement of the Ford claim. The result was a rapid loss of confidence by the lenders (exacerbated, no doubt, by a previous non-disclosure which had recently come to light to which we refer in Chapter 4, paragraph 4.9 below).

2.43   On 22 December 1999, HSBC offered revised short term financial facilities in light of the disclosures. The facilities offered were less than that projected as necessary by the group and its advisers. On 23 December 1999, Mr Carr and Mr Jeffrey resigned. On 24 December 1999 the remaining members of the board resolved to ask HSBC to appoint receivers and to suspend trading in TransTec's shares. Trading in TransTec shares was suspended on 24 December and the group was placed in administrative receivership beginning on 29 December 1999.

Shareholders

2.44   At the date of the appointment of receivers Mr Robinson remained the largest individual shareholder. After him, the shares were held by institutional investors and some were held by the directors or former directors. Mr Carr, for example, had a holding of approximately 1.5% of the issued share capital.

CHAPTER 3: THE FORD CLAIM

Introduction

3.1   We have set out in brief in Chapter 2 how the Ford claim arose and its settlement in August 1997 on the basis that Ford would be paid US $18 million in compensation, spread over three years. We have also reported on the non-disclosure of the existence of this settlement.

3.2   In this Chapter we deal with the accounting consequences of that claim and the compensation payments.

Non-Disclosure

3.3   Shortly after the claim was brought to the attention of TransTec it was determined to keep the matter as confidential as possible. The claim and its treatment was given a code name: "Project Durham". No non-executive directors were involved.

3.4   The 1996 accounts of TransTec were signed off on 25 April 1997. The 1996 accounts of TransTec Campsie were also dated as having been signed off on 25 April 1997. The existence of Ford's claim, as set out in their letter of 23 April 1997, was not disclosed in the 1996 accounts as an actual or contingent liability of either company. Nor was the settlement of the claim recognised in the 1997 accounts nor expressly recognised in the 1998 (the last) annual audited accounts of either company (nor indeed of any group company) as a charge against profits or liability in the balance sheet.

3.5   Further, until December 1999, it would appear that, despite opportunities to do so either directly or through announcement, accounts, annual reports, interim statements or public circulars, neither the fact of the claim, its settlement, nor the true reasons for the related payments to Ford were reported to the non-executive directors (including the successive chairmen of the group), to the auditors, the stock exchange, the group's lenders or brokers nor to the group's creditors, customers or shareholders and no notification under paragraphs 9.1 and 9.2 of the Listing Rules was made (see paragraph 1.5 above).

3.6   From the moment when TransTec received Ford's letter of 23 April 1997, apart from the opportunities for informing the non-executive directors, the opportunity for consideration of wider disclosure and dissemination arose on a number of occasions including via or through the group or subsidiary accounts (1996, 1997 and 1998), annual reports, interim statements (1997), and the public circulars issued on the acquisition of BSK Holdings Ltd (July 1996), Vector Plastics Ltd (July 1997) and CREMSA and ENSA (January 1998). On each such occasion the executive directors with knowledge of the Ford claim and its settlement would have had the opportunity to make disclosure but did not until, as we have said, December 1999. These are the bare facts; whether it was right not to have made such disclosure, the justification offered to us for not having done so and the identification of those responsible we will leave for our final report.

Debit Notes

3.7   We have already reported in Chapter 2 how the manner in which Ford was to recover the $18 million was by a system of debit notes allocated across the group to four different sites or subsidiaries including, but not limited to, TransTec Campsie.

3.8   Some £3 million of debit notes were received dated in 1997. These were explained to accounting staff at the relevant locations and to the auditors as premature charges relating to 1998. They were carried forward as prepayments in the balance sheet and not charged against profits for 1997. In this manner the profits of 1997 were mis-stated. The first year in which the settlement of the Ford claim affected TransTec's reported profits was 1998, when approximately £5.3 million was charged as an exceptional item. Another £1.9 million was capitalised in the balance sheet as a contribution to the cost of tooling. The total, £7.2 million, represented $12 million of the agreed $18 million compensation retained by Ford by the end of 1998. That left $6 million to be paid in 1999. As previously indicated, this $6 million was not recognised in the 1998 accounts.

3.9　　In 1999 on the somewhat belated arrival of the debit notes covering the remaining instalment payments of compensation, TransTec, owing to its financial difficulties, asked Ford to cancel or defer the outstanding $6 million. Ford were inclined to defer payment, but not to cancel the debit notes. The matter was still being negotiated when the group collapsed.

CHAPTER 4: MISCELLANEOUS OTHER MATTERS

Other Potential Accounting Irregularities

4.1   In addition to the matters to which we refer in this interim report, there are other matters regarding TransTec's accounting practices which require explanation. Since we have not yet concluded our investigations in this area, we have not dealt with them all at this stage beyond giving an indication of some of our concerns.

4.2   Our investigations of TransTec's accounting practices indicate, amongst other things, that there had been a tendency either to anticipate profits on contracts or to defer expenditure to future periods within the scope of available accounting policies. In other words, TransTec's accounting had tended to be "aggressive". Another way of putting that is to say that a more conservative view could have been taken of profits. Our other concerns include the descriptions or euphemisms given to various items in the accounts (including the payment of the debit notes which followed settlement of the Ford claim). Our present concern is that the accounts, at least from 1996 onwards, may have contained items that were mis-stated.

4.3   In July 1997 TransTec made a payment to Rover of £400,000 ostensibly as part of the 1997 cost down arrangements with Rover. TransTec's management seem to have regarded the payment as being made to secure a contract for a new project, known as the NG4 sump. The precise nature of this payment is not yet clear to us. When the payment was made no definite contract for the sump was, so far as we are aware, in existence. The payment was designated in TransTec's accounts as an advance payment for tooling (albeit no tooling actually existed at the time), apparently so that it did not have to be written off against profits. Our investigations into this matter are continuing.

The Earby Pension Fund

4.4   The 1994 and 1995 accounts of Earby revealed that an actuarial valuation of the pension scheme had taken place on 6 April 1993. The scheme assets were valued at some £3.275

million covering 88% of accrued benefits. The company was recommended to increase its contributions.

4.5 The 1996 accounts revealed that a further actuarial valuation had taken place on 6 April 1996. Although the scheme assets had now risen to some £4.138 million the cover of accrued benefits had decreased to 82%. Again the company was recommended to increase its contributions still further.

4.6 The 1997 and 1998 accounts disclosed a still further valuation had taken place on 5 April 1997. The level of cover of accrued benefits had by now dropped to 76%. Again increased contributions were recommended.

4.7 The shortfall at this stage was some £1.2m. In late 1999 a further valuation revealed that the shortfall had increased to £2.8m.

4.8 We have viewed these matters with some concern and our investigations into this aspect of the affairs of the group are still continuing. Tentatively, however, we are at present inclined to think that the shortfall was caused by changes in statutory minimum funding requirements and the relatively poor performance of life policies compared with equities, a large part of the scheme assets being invested in the former.

4.9 There is, however, one footnote to this matter. On 2 December 1999 Close Brothers, the group's advisers, were informed of the existence of this shortfall, since Earby was then in the course of being sold. Close Brothers expressed concern that they had not been informed of this matter before. They sought undertakings that there were no other undisclosed or contingent liabilities which they received. The revelation a short time later of the Ford claim came, as it were, to be the final nail in the coffin.

Causes and Reasons for Collapse

4.10 It is still too soon to form any definitive conclusion as to the reason for the collapse of the group. It is reasonably clear that the disclosure of the Ford claim was the proximate cause of the collapse but there are other reasons more complex and diverse: the decline in margins and volumes, the drain on cash resources and other matters on which we have not yet formed final conclusions and with which we will deal in our final report.

APPENDIX 1 : LIST OF ABBREVIATIONS

TransTec group

C&S	Central & Sheerwood plc
TransTec	TransTec plc
TransTec Campsie	TransTec Automotive (Campsie) Limited
A L Dunn	A L Dunn & Co Limited
Coventry Apex	Coventry Apex Engineering Company Limited
BEW	B.E.W. (Auto Products) Limited
Fenworth	Fenworth Limited
BSK	BSK Aluminium Limited
Earby	Earby Light Engineers Limited
CREMSA	Construcciones Radio Electro-Mecanicas Sistemas de Automocion SL
ENSA	Estampaciones Noroeste SA

Other companies

Ford	The international group of companies generally known as Ford Motor Company and/or individual members of that group, as the context requires
Rover	Rover Group Ltd
AlliedSignal	AlliedSignal Limited
HSBC	HSBC Bank plc
Close Brothers	Close Brothers Corporate Finance Limited

Other

The receivers	The joint administrative receivers of TransTec plc
SOHC	single overhead cam